Politics or Disease, please...

poems by

Sean J. Mahoney

Finishing Line Press
Georgetown, Kentucky

Politics or Disease, please...

Copyright © 2022 by Sean J. Mahoney
ISBN 978-1-64662-847-6 First Edition
All rights reserved under International and Pan-American Copyright Conventions. No part of this book may be reproduced in any manner whatsoever without written permission from the publisher, except in the case of brief quotations embodied in critical articles and reviews.

ACKNOWLEDGMENTS

Occupoetry ("In the Country")
Wordgathering ("Cnditions: Part I", "Cnditions: Part II"…originally published as "Conditions", Paint that Wagon I, Handles #41 (Blood Brain Barrier—Conflict with Contrast)")
Indolent Books / What Rough Beast ("He did not fall alone")
Right Hand Pointing ("The Fire Triangle—Oxygen")
Magnolia Review ("The Fire Triangle—Fuel, Heat")
Open Thought Vortex Magazine ("Hypomania")
Poets Reading the News ("The Sheltering Workshops", "No Fix Forthcoming", "The Red & the Black")
Tayo Literary Magazine ("When Body was a Black Lung")
Main St. Rag ("When We were a cub reporter")
The Fear of Monkeys ("When He was an arctic sea")
Rogue Agent ("1.14.18")
Kaleidoscope Magazine ("Marketable Phenomena");
Nine Mile Magazine ("Woe to the Crips", "And that is why too")

Publisher: Leah Huete de Maines
Editor: Christen Kincaid
Cover Art: Sean J Mahoney
Author Photo: Lady Dianne Mahoney
Cover Design: Elizabeth Maines McCleavy

Order online: www.finishinglinepress.com
also available on amazon.com

Author inquiries and mail orders:
Finishing Line Press
PO Box 1626
Georgetown, Kentucky 40324
USA

Table of Contents

In the Country 1

Cnditions: Pt. I 2

This Tuesday 3

He did not fall alone 4

Paint that Wagon I 5

The Fire Triangle 7

Hypomania 8

The Red & the Black 10

No Fix Forthcoming 13

Figurement 15

Paint that Wagon II 16

When Body was a black lung 19

When you needed the work 20

When We were a cub reporter 21

When He was an artic sea 22

1.14.18 23

Cnditions: Pt. II 25

Marketable Phenomena 26

The Sheltering Workshops 28

Woe to the Crips 30

And that is why too 32

Handles #41 (Blood Brain Barrier—Conflict with Contrast) 33

Paint that Wagon VIII 36

In the Country
    (spirit of Larry Levis)

My country greased civility.

My country embraces meme
and wraps superficial round
its skinnying shoulders.
My country cannot see straight
for it is triggers and magazines.
And that is aspic. And tongue.
And a lark. My country lives
in detours and is no longer
ours, no longer what my love
and I invented.

At the table we weep for our country
that it may one day grow to love
itself, its characters and wilds.
Our country believes in collections
rather than birds and smoke.
Our country cannot see crumbling
streets for the buildings of neon
wrap my country's bones in
dizzying light.

My love and I watch the foolish hand
stir the collective and change the topic.

My love and I hunch together
wondering how we lost it.

Cnditions: Part I

Forgive me for talking and talking. I took that what
Given me. Body: what I knew as normal is instead now
diagnosed and unfamiliar, foreign even and of a shifting
manner I cannot wrap my fingers around, cannot fathom,
for my ability to reason is based on slow rain I can smell
and the sight of blood loosed by thorns.

Word after word. I am not wholly autoimmune. I am sickness;
pre-existing. I slide and grasp. Whatever all I've got is it.
Bit by bit, hardly perceptible essences have been issued papers,
been shuttered without so much as a blanket or customary drink.

I carry the organs with me into what may be my star turn astride
a steed set against the fading glow of the horizon. I should be
working more with resistance, my country being how it is now.

I rest my head in my arms wondering why couldn't I
have won a piñata instead? But disease? Am I bound, too,
to the disability movement with this practiced, awkward
approach in how I re-wear worn fabrics, replay lost dialogues

…with the subtracting dead? Yes…messy. Yes.

This Tuesday

Nothing of significance happened on this day, this Tuesday, according to my head of holes and wires with bites. Was told by a 4-year old boy that he had been executed as a man, that his experience mirrored the country where he was snuffed out. Who would ice me with a condition?

Nothing of significance happened on this day, this Tuesday. Such were the relays down my wires of bytes. Memories serve and nothing more, nothing less. Faulty, fraudulent, and these children continue appearing as relays of the faults beneath our streets, the fraud—a failed state called home.

I read a scathing article by the Disabled and Deaf Uprising community responding to this or that AWP mess. How again the disability community got ignored and/or talked over and/or talked through and just outright shaded.

Neruda found a different, accelerated voice after Fascism moved in, after Lorca was shot, after the poppies were dried and ground up and sold as candy and the incinerated bones of the sacrificed were sprinkled out atop oatmeal and soup.

I read on. Outlaw poetry. Defiance and shame. Defiance. Shame. Possibly too much mother. I read about rhinos dying. I read of demonstrations and waiting, breath-holding for 6 minutes and 20 seconds…amid the swirl of notebooks and ammunition.

He did not fall alone

When He fell he did not fall alone.
And those others, those fallen crests,
hunt tirelessly. Not the weak, nor
the strong, the infirm or the young
will remain free so long as there be
swift confusion and babbling for truth.

It is promise serving blood pudding.
Promise filling the glass; more lead,
more tainted water. Promise allied
with a dead cold eye and a cruel hand
marking foreheads, starving the course
of being, stealing air and biting throats.

When He fell he did not fall alone.
Terror begat alerts which begat the bar
which begat the cell and finally prison.
Still the fallen came, hungering for that
pulse what was taken from garden and
from school and stripped from heartland.

They came for factory and union people.
By night they closed out the clerks, nurses
and watchmen. Impaling its public as well
as its servants the fallen broke the damn
place and left only a bold lie, germs getting
the double cross, & tiny crumbs.

Paint that Wagon I

Not just here…in this chilly place. I have procedures: MRIs, massages, acupuncture. I remove the leash and I wander. I wonder of the stewardship we ignore, of the crass confines of what used to be a romantic meadow but now belongs to the caged last polar bear and austere autocrat. Story lines involving miniature versions of myself, miniature to cellular level, racing through my very body searching for reason of a mind. But familiarity of sky scent is eerie…

We decided on the soup, which itself was modeled for the hangover. Noodles, savory broth. And we had some sparkling wine. I got a quick primer (sorry…I didn't know) on La Boheme and we were off to the opera and strangers for the next few hours. It's complicated…but we did touch once during the show… our fingertips. And no one the wiser. We know that there are people who know just about everyone…here and abroad… and communication is so 'lickety' these days that upsetting the wrong people would not be wise for those involved. No threat of violence mind you…but of humiliation and shame. All around. Better just to be careful. A friend of hers was also in attendance and seated to her right. I sat on her left. A single woman sat to my left. She is not my lover. The woman to my right however…I would sell my earrings to buy the doctor to save her life during any season…like Musetta…she is my, and I her…lover. Her name is poetry. Her name is pork belly. Chili-porn sauce. Star beam.

I believe that I am still dreaming. Same dream? Hallucinating even. Could my life have taken this wild turn without disease? Would I be sitting here writing this out if my body were abled?

The politics of rapid dancing drum up and down the hallways and low shafts, the dank, the dark before any splinter of light tells you release, shoot. And quiver. These episodes; no epiphanies, no guilt. During MRIs…think about a comic occasionally drawn in the head. It makes me laugh…you know, on the inside where it is said it counts more…which will delay arrival of the snake.

Thought of China's former 1-Child Policy. And infanticide. The question then becomes have global birth rates slowed at all in the last 50 years? Is this still the rage question that it once was? They are about half what they were 50 years ago. Is this pause, just us globally putting on the brakes and coming to terms with… this shit? A tactile scent. 1 Child…repercussions today. Many men. Forced marriages. Base culture. Breast wars continue and it cannot be said often enough that you will reap either one thing or another.

Imagine being shot down through a carotid artery and seeing blood cells from when you were 19, confused, and into punk. A cold heart. Imagine…$4000 holy water shoes…they still do say Jesus wept.

The Fire Triangle

<u>Oxygen</u>

Fill the room with it, with that air.
Fill the halls and the corridors,
the branches as it were. Bring us
all the lower explosive limits.

<u>Heat</u>

Raise all temperatures and create
sparks. Dialogue in ignition. Fan
suns and anything near bone,
near yesterday's familiar themes.

<u>Fuel</u>

Bring me your amassed trashes.
Bring your broken things and
lover's gifts. Give me food scraps
& used gauze—all that is expendable burns behind golden doors.

Hypomania

But I got into MS in my teens as I remember it. Just experimenting like everybody else I ran with at the time. I mean I tried a bunch of stuff then: coke, crack, red meat, wax paper, touches of AC, guitars of DC, banana peels, mind altering substances that were alteration in name only…that is until you shoveled in the moating. This MS smack literally re-stitched the make and the up and the wherewithal of *Am I?* Literally clustered my fuck. My ostensible reasons for rising. My old, buttered meditations of body and soul scratching. My purple.

It's funny they—that everybody else—can all still run now. And me? On MS 24/7. Just cannot give it up.

But it started more subtly…like I would indulge in MS at house parties in the bathroom with the host and a host of simply curious, or backstage at clubs with a couple of the players who always had the best stuff. Maybe me and the girl would sneak some MS back to her apartment and talk-talk TNT all night while doing it on the cold coffee table with the picture of Morrison pressed neatly underneath the glass …MS dusting that face.

But I have it now. Addiction, that is. And I can't stop. Like the MS shit too much. I'd just as soon let it tear through me than give it up. I have raked through the shag looking for specks and bits, licked the glass where we had lined MS out, fellated, degraded, toyed, stolen D's jewelry and my brother's children and sold one for another hit of my hard stem one. I have been to the meetings and danced the 12 steps over and over again until my legs gave way. I did sweats and saunas and streakings. Nothing changed except how I felt about the world writ large. I would push that place

away and bring it close once more. Over and over
until I dropped world one too many times and world
chipped. World complained about me and my kind
by way of infrastructure, glances and abnegations and
manuals; blatant obstacles. I would push that place
away again and then break and bring world close
like a comforting dear friend; once more feeling both
a natural end and beginning of what gets me off.

The Red & the Black

I rip music. Shostakovich complete trios
And sonatas. The case cover is red and
Black with an almost watermarked
Image of the hammer and sickle; labor
And peasantry. The value of my work
Exerted out tubes of my feet and into
Capital gains and capital cities and
Astonishing rates of return. I am a
Pill. I am a walking loving eating
Fucking opioid den.

Red and black. Turn back the clock:
Just say no we are told. Again.
Don't take any drugs ever. Look
The other way. Give yourself over
To scripture or golf just as Dimiti
Respun his work around government
News frenzies designed for and by
Malevolent denigration. You see
The problem is not with the company
But with your weakness. Your tone
Difference.

Take your medicine. Refill and use.
Demand pain, scream out of opaque
States that you just need a little
Pick up. Julien Sorel, master of love
And lover of armed forces mistook
Steps of ascension but had he had
Opioids, the church of a narcotic
Sanctuary perhaps then and only
Then would his plot twists have
Yielded material gains for state,
For church, his Eros proletariat.

I rip music. Shostakovich. The tremor
And violence of Piano Trio No.2
Rattles my bones as I am sure no
Doubt the romantic swells of an
Overdose feel to all affected by
Such horrible accidents. So easy
It is. So casual is this ease with which
We prescribe and ingest and take
And take again. Never more than
A few hours without medicating,
Never more than a phone call,
A visit, a hopeful whimper as
This thing we call life has gotten
Almost comical and ridiculous:
Opium. Morphine. Behold heroin.
Cocaine. Greet methamphetamine.
Finally see the wolves; call them
Tinkering gods, pulse manipulators
Rubbing every one of our buttons
Just the right way.

No clean line here. No smooth face.
No graceful resolution of theme.
Chaos and disenchantment. Plead
For more. Plead to make it all go away.
Ask for forgiveness. Bury your anger
In the music you produce. Walk.
Negate love. Julien Sorel—bounce
Your way into church, refuse Counsel.
Comfort the masters. One way or
the other your heart will be taken
from you, taken and punctured.

Psychosis of literature and throb of
Competing tone voices pulling your
Skin apart, the red and the black,
Blood army of pills and bruise church
Of sedation. The hammer, the sickle,
The labor of breathe, molestation
Of a regular peasant stripping down
And getting into bed with the wolf.

No Fix Forthcoming

It has been suggested—perhaps not too often—
'tis better to bleed kneeling than cower on
your feet. Let your red love ooze before you,
before facing autophagia of god & country.
Water cannons at your back, glass ceiling in eyes.
Discover long after this new set of facts that you
parsed expendable poetry for the many twerks and
insecurities of history. Picture books showing
you pulling train cars with your teeth while
publicly getting them kicked out by your own
elected public servants. They who swore an oath
to silence, pledged allegiance to confusion,

got to work years ago burning the legs out from
under a republic upon which we now stand
like an idea of life, of living at all, even mattered.
Meek with masks and sick buried in cold clock
towers trucks buildings, their death of form
supplicating itself before gravity and reckless
authority; to them for whom symbolism has no
meaning beyond what simply transacts moment
to moment, restroom to restroom; to them children
standing before tanks, waving at the drones. And
to those watching all day news telenovelas, eating
black licorice, buying outlawed books: how can any
be so sure this is not really as it is, and how erasure
always has been all along?

This place demoralized me, bade me bite the apple
all for chalking a simple flower on a people's wall.

I do not see myself surviving convenience nor
the convergence of autocrats and oil. I do not
believe in desperate page turning and printer's ink
thumbprints as though water or war be words worthy

of my conceit; but all will swallow, shall broke perish
in skin folds like the liquid run of these new lost boys
who will never know quite how close the sword came
before their red, ripe young throats.

Past aged governmental outposts, this chirping brain
of pious evangelical myopia, out the bar-coded
barrier doors into pugilist America blood puddles
on every corner. Teeth in each gutter. Financially
cold hatred has had its cloak revoked, its clothing
removed, and finds itself planted in yards and public
spaces and set aflame before the cameras. And while
the decades of loose trust and fashionable lie singe
and cinder off…this creature does not die so willingly.
Listen carefully, book burning at first light, and hear
irregular breathing as this creature strives to remain
wealthy for the skies, out of sight, just hardly alive.

Across parking lots full of cars and airplanes, dossiers,
irregular fruits, congressional candy, school lunch
programs, and backwards into a thick cloud, the land
promises scars and repeated layers of thrown monies,
rubber bullets, malfeasance. Hacking cough ignored.
Brushed aside. An unrelenting cough. What can you
not afford to not say or not do?

So very little gained after it all.

The sun sets again, the moon rises, and few stars
are visible above the metropolitan light spectacles
on the ground. What is normal gets shadier and
less fair—tangled like the dusty world's hair—
against white noise of the 24/7 horizon.

(*italics*—Time Spirals by Kenneth Rexroth)

Figurement

Narrative cost; an idea of cripped fairy tales, vile archetypes
Before clear cement sets and I see earth beneath myself
Disappearing in quick air, my molecules disappearing as
Milliseconds into other timelines, full phobias of triumph,
Slicked embrace of wet ironic metaphors. Difficult though
To say politely without intent; the tongue does its best work
When untethered from polite conversation. But a hall with
Which to house a disability dialogue remains playfully
Elusive, downright stubborn. This dialogue does not require
Another hope symposium. Life and good times have been so
Plentiful, so easy for bumping the lanes of those with blue,
Those with clay in their veins; being possessed flat-out
Sucks; part of those desk-sets, as disposable as strands of
Your hair upon my shoulder pointing me any other way.

Paint that Wagon II

Imagine. Imagine seeing your life in platelets. Cells. Your epic moments. Illustrative defeats. We are done talking about battles for the moment…although honestly, this situation we find ourselves in currently—being shot down the neck via the carotid artery—is indeed the result of a battle. Running from our immune system(s). This crush of AD (Autoimmune Disease) is fast catching up to the global We, in that the numbers are well above what one would describe as staggering. Like we're talking amounts of money that far exceed the costs of Cancer.

Cancer Girl's Hair Set on Fire is a poem I did years ago. The 'idea event' happened in 2004. In Wales. "*I'm a cancer. Cancer is a menace. Cancer is corporate. Cancer is conceived.*" And yet Cancer is a star. Like many diseases…you won't notice. Those tiny, tiny clots get thrown; insulin is not produced, lungs not kept healthy, the vanishing myelin, build-up of plaque, opacity of the familiar.

Accountability Formation, or just formation, is an army term reiterating the chain of command. Status of soldiers. Location of soldiers. But…Where are my mom and her sister now? The older sister is dying and they are driving her across country so she can pass in Palm Springs in the company of her younger sister. Yeah, Faulkner-esque. But first there is much to be done in New Rochelle where Auntie D has lived for at least 40 years; accounts to close and cancel; merchandise for selling or trade, before they can head west.

Mom will be the final sib living having said so long to big brother years ago.

"*Babies are conceived. Ideas are born in moments of duress. Why* "*Cancer Girl?*"

A cartoon I sometimes animate in my head while undergoing this or that. So my characters, my Id, Ego, and Super Idiot characters, are being shot down the carotid artery in a quick move to evade evisceration by them damn renegade T-cells. Those simpletons—the white blood cells—narrated the escape. You see these pitiless cretins had trouble accepting the idea of psyche denizens racing along the body freeways as though entitled to all-access permeability. Service to the body politic. So these characters get dumped as though refuse through the artery wall and whoosh… gone. Escaping to the heart…for further distribution. Will the three be separated? Outlook unclear…this was bound to get interesting…this process. A story? And what…of politics. Shall we dismantle the emperor? Falsely execute more bears?

(postscript confession: this last paragraph has the words simpletons and cretins within it. An editor friend pointed out that use of such words around the disability community could be problematic. It gave me pause. Had I committed an ableism? Was I guilty of taking my people for granted, taking us as disposable and flexible around all manner of objectification tossed upon our crip-playground? Or there's…I am part of this damn community…this damn community. I consulted the OED. To read the variations, the interpretations. So I rewrote it:

Those rash and myopic white blood cells narrated their escape; creeps having trouble accepting the idea of psyche denizens racing along the body freeways as though entitled to all-access permeability. Service to the body politic.
And then reached out to the East Coast for counsel. Another editor friend. She suggested, and I'll paraphrase here, fuck it. And so I changed it back again. So…what is correct play?)

The lover. Kissing during bath sessions is like punctuation for our dialogues. Kissing is a means of transportation…this commerce of tongues. She takes a long drink of sparkling wine and leans in. We kiss and the wine is swished between our mouths; cavities cradling the curios of civilization and spit swapping glory. Fingers

hide and Elvis sings of girls so like candy. Yet nobody wants to talk about voting rights. We've gotten very good at this. We have had many years of practice.
I love wife more than air. And will. And she me. We aren't compelling creatures.

"Bianca Powell was in a corridor at Pontarddulais Comprehensive when her hair, which had grown back after four years of chemotherapy, was set alight. A 14-year-old boy has been bailed pending further inquiries."

What else is there to ask? This type of politeness infuriates. And it persists today. It's like the "Top men" comment at the end of the first Indiana Jones movie…*Oh nevermind the details will just bore you*…So bore me. Tell me what I do not want to hear. Tell me why you are focused more on slowing progression, re-routing, temporarily pacifying, rather than finding out why AD happens. Surely there are triggers and…my favorite…'underlying reasons'…but let's say in the case of MS…why? We want a rationality to the process…

Microbiota…A good word…Confident…Structurally sound. Vowel heavy.

But this diversion speaks little in the ways and means of motive. What are you trying to impart to Cancer Girl young man? Has she not suffered well enough? Do you think she has had her first kiss yet? Has she bled yet? Do you believe she daydreams of Prince and doves crying? Do you think she made a choice for cancer—arms opening for Cancer as it stood trenchcoated, bowler in hand at the front door? I hope you get hit by a double-decker bus little prick. Why am I stuck on this event from 15 years ago…so distant…what lingers in the wind is nothing new.

It is recirculating by line by…

When Body was a black lung

You, Body, crushed me with disease.
An earmark & a toehold disease.
A disease beholden to coal: formerly
jolly, innocent, and sparkled emblem
of fossil products. A lung-load of dust.
Those days of carts streaming in and
out of tunnels full of black gold
have been on the wane for decades
now. I would have you point
your gnarled fingers at the party
crucified as anti-energy but that
is not a complete story. This myth
changes as often as the bulb in
a headlamp. You would not bring
yourself forth to admit sickness else
lose your job—that is how soundly
your country loves you, how it
breaks its back for you. And you,
dirty and toiling in its bowels.
Earth releases its shit before
your pick. You Body have soiled
decency. There is no service medal
for your sacrifice. No your kids
get put out and your home is
taken. When you try and fill in
an application the paper is blacked
from your coughing of Kentucky
and Virginia and Ohio. Coal is not
coming back and what little
remains resides inside you.
This the tolling bell, for whom
you once did serve when you
could breathe enough to rise each
day in darkness and return home
darker than the night itself. These
tones of silica embedded upon me
weighing each breath like a false
sense of security, like a white towel
waving over a filthy promise.

When you needed the work

When you needed the work
But turned it down, had to,
So as to qualify for that SSI;
That savings account steady
As a descent, a dive long head
Burst of hopeful idea and
Sang froid dripping from pores
Awash with your tummy tuck.

Several of you planted fruit
Trees and tomatoes in the back
In planter boxes with drip water.
But weary of just getting out
Of bed alone anymore, fearing
How much longer this will go on;
Pull bones out of beds, dirty
Them with labor and with ache
In a chair at home where you
Ate, and where you will pass.

When We were a cub reporter

When We wrote this first story about the rapidly disappearing bee populations and efforts aimed at boosting those very same vanishing winged queens and workers We could not realize—for we were but a cub, and humble though we would most times forget to be—that We indeed created a metaphor for post-truth, for post-real and post-equality, for post-transparency, for Post Cereals and post-hole digger, for post coital and post-postal service. For post-service.

Service developed a weak heel. Service grew cancerous. Service fell victim. Service suffered multiple stabbings. Service developed spots. Service plunged to all-time lows. Service yelled and pouted. Service refused irrefutable facts. Service played. Service stopped calling these deceits out.

But We felt the call. Felt the real truth swimming our breast not the bloody truth scooping our sockets. We culled information. We library-ed. We widely read. We asked questions and respected sources. Walked pavements. Beat the tools. Scooped the scoop and left bullshit piled at the door.

When We were a cub reporter We were eager reporting and alert while shuffling in the streets. We wrote in the cafes and bars using the beat tools, the tried and true savvy.

So strike the streets and report non-stop how the land got where sickened service is now…We reportedly said.

When He was an arctic sea

When He was cold and grey beneath overcast
Skies bloated with rain satellites mistook his
Pallor for deep blue. For fierce calm and strident
Peace. Would that it were so, that eyes took notice.

A select few knew what heap lolled beneath air
Mass and skyscape, lightening and feathers as
Nonplussed as salt crystals forming in eyelashes.
A few knew that trillions of diatoms and plankton

Prepped long caution chains across all bodies
Of water. He had lusting days augmented by drill
Bits, by gushing sewer pipes, by harpoons and
Plastic islands. Retribution arrived, struck lethal

Blows, walleted sweet and sour capital at the expense
Of all things offered before it. Had He been a man
He would have wept at the savagery. Had He
Been a man after having such regret cannoned into

His mouth he would revoke all life origins for such
A slight. He, pocked and thick, instead sponged
Ashore gently as if a harmless manatee, practicing
Slow breathing exercises, short cuts and parasitic

Lamprey tactics. Would that He were useful, that eyes
Took notice of black mayonnaise pluming ashore.

1.14.18

Finagling the vocal cadence of one Nancy Mairs
As I tell you about last evening in the dog
Park with our pups. I had the three of them.
We were a quarter through our stay when from
Some chamber within a valve failed. And
The urge was upon me. And what happens
Happens. God had nothing to do with *it*.
I cannot say for sure that the MS had
Anything to do with it either. Perhaps *it*
Was just me not being prepared prior
To leaving home. We ran out, me and the
Pups. They get excited when they see me
With the keys and leading them out the door.
They know and their excitement is contagious.
So we're lolling around the park, the smallest
Stays near me if there are many pups
Shooting and darting around. The other two
Play. I begin looking for anyplace around
That might afford a moment of discretion.
Tis not to be; not here, not now. I talk
To myself silently: suck *it* up buttercup.
We're almost done here. And that works
For awhile. Until the dogs are re-leashed
And we are out the gate headed back toward
The Subaru. I sense a few small releases.
I know there are no clothes in the car but
I have plastic shit mitts provided by the park.
The dogs are loaded and I get in, fish a bag
Out of my pockets and cram it down between
My legs and under my crotch. Is this MS?
There really is no way to know for sure.
How can I make claims of a disease with an
Entire predilection resting upon unpredictable
And erratic timing. All have had that moment
Of near bursting. Everyone has leaked. A little.

A lot. Be *it* the truth. Be *it* the pee. Be *it*
Brain function. The whistle is internal. Spot
On the front of my shorts upon returning
Home was not: bottom of a coffee mug shape.
Khaki shorts. Should have worn the Uniglo
Briefs—thicker cotton. How can we ever
Appreciate that what happens, happens.
Today the leaks? Tomorrow Montecito
Disappears into a much darker sorrow.

Cnditions: Part II

People with MS relative to total global population: .000343%.

My hijacked auto-functions are not connecting themselves as circled wagons. No the orgy ensuing tremors when magnetically resonated. My community of tissue is being systematically divided. The targeted disruption proving quite a viable strategy. My community becoming smaller.

These conductions I internally emit—next to invisible and near a sadness in more than 99% of the world often lose their way. My hand extended to grasp yours. A gift in...
...yes that signal, that electrical itch falling in a stairway rose well, set forth, and could not be re-received today. No more deconstruct, abuse, partially rebuild. Repeat. Pass on.

Once I have stopped talking, momentarily, for pondering the amusing; this vast frailty. We dissimilar animals jockeying, ramming our crests for a ticket; stamped as a geeked feature.

Marketable Phenomena

We, you and I, fail in communicating but not in embracing.
Intertwined we are. Spooky caduceus. Release me. Allow
me release of satisfactory breath. Please release my chest.
Halting astonishment and struggle? You bestow this upon
me. For all our misunderstandings I have never denied
your superstar status; how spectacular you are lobe by lobe.
When I see you refracted through my pupil, spread on fibrous
white matter blankets, resting yourself after the brain pillage
I am convinced that perhaps, over time, we can negotiate
territory like Lidwina, R; Pryor, and Jacqueline du Pre.

I take a tablespoon of concentrated black licorice root once
a week, just to see if I can in turn cause you recoil, or even
draw you out of my northern poles. And though resolute
magnets can track your maps, the papery places you have
tagged, committed crimes in and spread your gospels
of systematic disruption, I feel as if we are left no choice
but remaining strangers on a train, me groping for murder
weapons, my missing and/or damaged strings and impartially
random broken bits of family tree. I find you dramatically
indifferent to my desires considering how frequently I stave
off poems and body art projects for purely incomprehensible
reasons: knee jerk reactions to what I no longer have and, or,
maybe, drunk dialing people I have convinced myself that I
need commune with—like Lidwina, R. Pryor and Jacqueline
du Pre—for growth. Long dead people.

Seriously? What is the angle?

My angel you confuse. As if your distinct alliterate persuasion
gives you a certain luxury, a piss-poor mastery over gravity
and therefore over floors beneath me. If I started wearing tin
foil hats would that totally prevent communications with
the mother-fuck-me ship? Prevent my falling like Lidwina,

R. Pryor, and Jacqueline de Pre? If that be the case then
I will, from here until my last breath, consider you more
a series of nuisances rather than my marketable phenomena.

The Sheltering Workshops

Once canopies caught fire the quick to rescind
Olmstead burst into red-taped mummies screaming
For regulations to kindle-spark along with them.

Provisions existed for many long-haired moons
Whereby those with what bureaucratic masses
Termed deformities and/or singular shortcomings

Would work segregated from regular normies,
Would work for less than the carrots and straw
Asses make each day. These changes brought

To us all by thin-lipped and tight fingered
Organizations with rough-hewn names like
ACCSES and Department of Justice, monikers

Akin to elbow calluses, bare knee patches and
Exploitive workplaces and sub-minimum wage
Soul leeching. These changes made in sessions

Framed by coin and greenback. Yes, one can
Always follow the money; look for the mangled
Bodies of the disabled under the armored car.

They say you are so not worthy of the same
Protections cocooning the able-bodied. They
Blow their noses on the bold text of the ADA.

They justify the sheltered workshop as training
Grounds for those many who would have no
Other chance is this beautifully cruel world.

No chance to reach their full potential. Here we
Have the ugly catch-1, catch-2 of entitlement,
The full bloom of embarrassment for the rigging

Shows, the magnets and slow springs, the fractions
Of seconds. Arcade. Fire for those born with wires
crossed, knotted, or often times missing entirely...

Woe to the Crips

Woe to the crips of the badass
man's land; woe to their knees
and wheels. Blessed the throttled
of voice and damp of ear, sing
of sights ne'er bore witness to
and wipe that smirk away, wipe
the spittle from the wired chin
for there are no actors to play
you or you or even you.

Woe to the crips of the land!
Woe to the tubes and varied
buckles. Blessed be those who
refuse acknowledging our
spectacle of ramps in disrepair
and a Net given over to muzzlers
and palm greasers; that sludge
could fuel my iron lung, my
eleven pacemakers, my power
chair, my 57th MRI. But no,
though they may take my lane
they cannot seduce, no longer
lay claim to my bullshit taxes.
I want to know for once
where my dollars are going,
who they buy and what they
are keeping quiet with trach
tubes. I know they breath not
for me; know even relayed
via faults in my wiring, faults
in my wiring, faults…
…somewhere along the line
      an error

in sequencing got made, made me
less than a textbook definition of…

Woe to the crips who wake with
outrage, who seethe and roar as
big pockets water golf courses
inaccessible for people like us: we
stake the abled to shrubs, around
greens, alongside walkable pathways
…acknowledging shared spectacle.

And that is why too

What happened moments, even decades, ago may as well
Not have happened at all. Spots of sticky disbelief
Linger about thighs and belly. Out comes relevant. Seed
A used husk. Transitions. Transmission needling slowly
Into wet wired spaces. Unwilling and prone in treason
Yet a residue remains. A lean fatigue in tote to be sure, all
While humming 337 variations of Buckdancer's Choice.

Find it all ridiculously sour: blame the broken system,
Blame the token incentives and the incessant pressure.
Point at the balloons in the sky, point at tacos and food
On illuminated boards. Say anything to fix this body.

Lean sadness. Knowing finally that I will not walk
On smoother water ever again but with the addition
Of salts nor will I sink below. As the ways and means
Of handling dysfunction make themselves known
Day in, day out, I recall long drives speeding through
The Santa Cruz mountains in the Catalina, the V8
Block under hood urgently churning valley dust and
Grits of coast sand upward as if ejaculated art, singing
Now of panic and gut measured response. I become
What happens. I am animal and circuitry.

Handles #41
(Blood Brain Barrier—Conflict with Contrast)

I drive myself like
gadolinium seeking fissures.
I and myself fold and open.
I handle us well.
My doors are locked
and without handles.
I have family. I have friends
and doctors too, but this
is my ride. It would seem
that I am alone
to speeding motorists or
peace officers
save that blanketed
malady-free husk of me
leaning into the passenger
door and window.
It would seem that I have
a handle on my state, a grip
around the neck
of a causeless ailment.
So it would seem.

Meanwhile, the worlds
I hide behind words
are stuffed in the boot, struggling
with metaphors for nociceptive
and vagal response, trying
to still the vials of potions
almost as clear as my CSF.

And somewhere else—
Minneapolis, maybe—
snow pockets around ankles
slogging in the streets

(I imagine that that temperature
is bliss for someone like me).

My grandfather is there, possibly,
father of my father
and genetic marker of my nerves.
He babbles about which side
of the bed his trousers hung from.
Anyone who needs to be tapped
for what they were supposed
to be rather than what they are
can find this man, my grandfather,
and anyone can listen
to his stories about skylines
in NYC and the poetry he wrote.
He is there for those juiced up
on meds, for the lesions
perched and on a roll of coin
calculating the nerve
they have between tooth.
For those who curse their past
or the state of their present
and the issues with mobility
yet to come. There will be issues
no matter how still systems
seem. All there is is hope
so I'm slow on the road.
I yield to the signs
when I consider turns
as I had begun
eating myself.

I will light up the film again.
I will flare. Sometime.
For now I'm handling

as I glide Route 152
back to Santa Cruz.

Sky filled with driving light.
Moon creatures fix themselves
and wait for me to fly by.

Paint that Wagon VIII

A stage, a tight throng of people touching me,
shouting bro names. My girl at the time led me
away onto the hood of some car and just needed
me to hold her. Must be like that when all we
are are thoughts and prayers and slush monies.

Though one line by Rebecca Gayle H. plucks
my string theories. Why is this detail remarkably
unimportant? Why can't my leg stop spasming?
Is there rest in my future of any kind? Someone
please plead for me as well; my lips are swollen.

On backs of men and hips of women plague doctors
arrive in capes. Paid to do…what? Lie to suns, lie
with dramatic encounters and baseless denials. Zero
sum crisis…ashes, ashes we all may well be dead.
Where is my federal physician with requisite cold

heart and 8 icy fingers whisking my emotional
concern away, frying my doubt, buttering over
my right to be anywhere, packaging my nipples
as though selling me away, sensationally dumb
for the next stop, show, and anonymous hook-up.

Rain may clear the air for a spell.
Rain just might be viral for a spell.

www.ingramcontent.com/pod-product-compliance
Lightning Source LLC
LaVergne TN
LVHW041556070426
835507LV00011B/1124